My Super Official Spy Mission Book

The BEST Spy Mission Training
Book for Kids!

SPY RULES:

1. Do NOT break any of your house rules while completing your missions.
2. Safety first! Abort mission if you or someone else could get hurt.
3. Be QUIET!
4. Do not get spotted, blend into your surroundings.
5. Do not scare your grown-up!
6. And finally, do not break any of these rules!

How to Play:

Hello and welcome!

During your training you will be completing different tasks to sharpen your spy skills. There are 4 levels, with 10 missions in each level to complete. Only after you complete one mission, may you move onto the next!

Think of a place as your "base", this can be a bedroom, corner, tent, etc. This space is your safe zone and you do not lose if you are spotted in this zone. If you are in the middle of a mission and things are getting hairy, ABORT, and return to your base! There is no limit to the amount of attempts you get for each mission.

Start with Level 1, Mission 1. Read and follow the directions. Be sure to bring your A-game, as the missions will get harder with each level.

Remember, spies must have good observational skills, creativity, flexibility, and the ability to blend into their surroundings.

Good Luck & Have Fun!

P.s. If you get stumped and need a mission item idea, see the idea list in the back of the book.

Your mission, should you choose to accept, is waiting.

Turn the page to begin.

LEVEL 1
MISSION 1
(Follow your instincts.)

Date:_____ **Time:**_____

MISSION:

1. Make your way from base to a busy room or area.

2. Spy something **BLACK**, then return to base and record your finding without being spotted!

My mission item is:

_____

Was the mission completed without getting caught?
YES   NO

If you were spotted, or the mission was aborted, wait 3 minutes then try again. You got this!

LEVEL 1
MISSION 2

(Blend in.)

Date:_____   Time:_____

MISSION:

1. Make your way from base to a busy room or area.

2. Spy something **PURPLE**, then return to base and record your finding without being spotted!

My mission item is:

_____

Was the mission completed without getting caught?
YES   NO

If you were spotted, or the mission was aborted, wait 3 minutes then try again. Keep Trying!

LEVEL 1
MISSION 3
(Shhhhhh.)

Date:_____ **Time:**_____

MISSION:

1. Make your way from base to a busy room or area.

2. Spy something **BLUE**, then return to base and record your finding without being spotted!

My mission item is:

_____

Was the mission completed without getting caught?
YES   NO

If you were spotted, or the mission was aborted, wait 3 minutes then try again. Spies never give up!

LEVEL 1
MISSION 4

(Assume Nothing.)

Date:_____ Time:_____

MISSION:

1. Make your way from base to a busy room or area.

2. Spy something **GREEN**, then return to base and record your finding without being spotted!

My mission item is:

_____

Was the mission completed without getting caught?
YES   NO

If you were spotted, or the mission was aborted, wait 3 minutes then try again. Waiting is a spy skill too!

LEVEL 1
MISSION 5

(Go with the flow.)

Date:_____   Time:_____

MISSION:

1. Make your way from base to a busy room or area.

2. Spy something **PINK**, then return to base and record your finding without being spotted!

My mission item is:

_____

Was the mission completed without getting caught?
YES   NO

If you were spotted, or the mission was aborted, wait 3 minutes then try again. Halfway to Level 2!

LEVEL 1
MISSION 6
(Over halfway to Level 2.)

Date:_____ **Time:**_____

MISSION:

1. Make your way from base to a busy room or area.

2. Spy something **BROWN**, then return to base and record your finding without being spotted!

My mission item is:

_____

Was the mission completed without getting caught?
YES   NO

If you were spotted, or the mission was aborted, wait 3 minutes then try again. Nice commitment!

LEVEL 1
MISSION 7
(Keep your options open.)

Date:_____ **Time:**_____

MISSION:

    1. Make your way from base to a busy room or area.

    2. Spy something **YELLOW**, then return to base and record your finding without being spotted!

My mission item is:

_____

Was the mission completed without getting caught?
YES   NO

If you were spotted, or the mission was aborted, wait 3 minutes then try again. Keep trying!

LEVEL 1
MISSION 8

(Take a deep breath.)

Date:_____ **Time:**_____

MISSION:

1. Make your way from base to a busy room or area.

2. Spy something **ORANGE**, then return to base and record your finding without being spotted!

My mission item is:

_____

Was the mission completed without getting caught?
YES   NO

If you were spotted, or the mission was aborted, wait 3 minutes then try again. You got this!

LEVEL 1
MISSION 9

(Act natural.)

Date:_____   **Time:**_____

MISSION:

1. Make your way from base to a busy room or area.

2. Spy something **RED**, then return to base and record your finding without being spotted!

My mission item is:

_____

Was the mission completed without getting caught?
YES   NO

If you were spotted, or the mission was aborted, wait 3 minutes then try again. One more to go!

LEVEL 1
MISSION 10
(ALMOST THERE!)

Date:_____ **Time:**_____

MISSION:

1. Make your way from base to a busy room or area.

2. Spy something **WHITE**, then return to base and record your finding without being spotted!

My mission item is:

_____

Was the mission completed without getting caught?
YES   NO

If you were spotted, or the mission was aborted, wait 3 minutes then try again.

CONGRATULATIONS!
You are now a
LEVEL 2 SPY!

LEVEL 2
MISSION 1
(Get ready to take it up a notch!)

Date:_____ **Time:**_____

MISSION:

1. Make your way from base to a room or an area.

2. Spy something both

ROUND & RED, then return to base and record your finding without being spotted!

My mission item is:

_____

Was the mission completed without getting caught?
YES   NO

If you were spotted, or the mission was aborted, wait 3 minutes then try again. You got this!

LEVEL 2
MISSION 2
(Remember your strengths.)

Date:_____ **Time:**_____

MISSION:

1. Make your way from base to a room or an area.

2. Spy something both **SQUARE & BROWN**, then return to base and record your finding without being spotted!

My mission item is:

_____

Was the mission completed without getting caught?
YES   NO

If you were spotted, or the mission was aborted, wait 3 minutes then try again. Spies never quit!

LEVEL 2
MISSION 3
(If all else fails, distract!)

Date:_____ Time:_____

MISSION:

1. Make your way from base to a room or an area.

2. Spy something both

RECTANGULAR & BLACK,

then return to base and record your finding without being spotted!

My mission item is:

_____

Was the mission completed without getting caught?

YES   NO

If you were spotted, or the mission was aborted, wait 3 minutes then try again. KEEP TRYING!

LEVEL 2
MISSION 4
(Remember your mission!)

Date:_____ **Time:**_____

MISSION:

1. Make your way from base to a room or an area.

2. Spy something both **LONG & WHITE**, then return to base and record your finding without being spotted!

My mission item is:

_____

Was the mission completed without getting caught?
YES   NO

If you were spotted, or the mission was aborted, wait 3 minutes then try again. Nice commitment!

LEVEL 2
MISSION 5

(Plan in secret.)

Date:_____ Time:_____

MISSION:

1. Make your way from base to a room or an area.

2. Spy something both **RECTANGULAR & BLUE**, then return to base and record your finding without being spotted!

My mission item is:

_____

Was the mission completed without getting caught?
YES   NO

If you were spotted, or the mission was aborted, wait 3 minutes then try again. Halfway to Level 3!

LEVEL 2
MISSION 6
(You are confident.)

Date:_____ **Time:**_____

MISSION:

1. Make your way from base to a room or an area.

2. Spy something both

RECTANGULAR & WHITE, then return to base and record your finding without being spotted!

My mission item is:

_____

Was the mission completed without getting caught?
YES   NO

If you were spotted, or the mission was aborted, wait 3 minutes then try again. Keep Going!

LEVEL 2
MISSION 7
(Don't forget to focus.)

Date:_____ Time:_____

MISSION:

1. Make your way from base to a room or an area.

2. Spy something **CLEAR**, then return to base and record your finding without being spotted!

My mission item is:

_____

Was the mission completed without getting caught?
YES   NO

If you were spotted, or the mission was aborted, wait 3 minutes then try again. Waiting is a spy skill too!

LEVEL 2
MISSION 8
(Practice grows your skills.)

Date:_____ **Time:**_____

MISSION:

1. Make your way from base to a room or an area.

2. Spy something **ROUND & ORANGE**, then return to base and record your finding without being spotted!

My mission item is:

_____

Was the mission completed without getting caught?

YES   **NO**

If you were spotted, or the mission was aborted, wait 3 minutes then try again. Keep it up!

LEVEL 2
MISSION 9
(You're getting the hang of this now.)

Date:_____ **Time:**_____

MISSION:

1. Make your way from base to a room or an area.

2. Spy something **GOLDEN**, and then return to base and record your finding without being spotted!

My mission item is:

_____

Was the mission completed without getting caught?
YES   NO

If you were spotted, or the mission was aborted, wait 3 minutes then try again. One more to go!

LEVEL 2
MISSION 10
(Almost there!)

Date:_____ Time:_____

MISSION:

1. Make your way from base to a room or an area.

2. Spy something both **ROUND & SILVER**, then return to base and record your finding without being spotted!

My mission item is:

_____

Was the mission completed without getting caught?
YES   NO

If you were spotted, or the mission was aborted, wait 3 minutes then try again.

CONGRATULATIONS!
You are now a
LEVEL 3 SPY!

LEVEL 3
MISSION 1
(The fun is just getting started!)

Date:_____   Time:_____

MISSION:

1. Make your way from base to a room or an area.

2. Spy something **YOU CAN THROW**, and then return to base and record your finding without being spotted!

My mission item is:

_____

Was the mission completed without getting caught?
YES   NO

If you were spotted, or the mission was aborted, wait 3 minutes then try again. Too easy!

LEVEL 3
MISSION 2
(Overcome challenges.)

Date:_____ **Time:**_____

MISSION:

1. Make your way from base to a room or an area.

2. Spy something both

SMOOTH & FLAT, then return to base and record your finding without being spotted!

My mission item is:

_____

Was the mission completed without getting caught?
YES   NO

If you were spotted, or the mission was aborted, wait 3 minutes then try again. Waiting is a spy skill too!

LEVEL 3
MISSION 3

(You have what it takes!)

Date:_____ **Time:**_____

MISSION:

1. Make your way from base to a room or an area.

2. Spy something that feels **ROUGH**, and then return to base and record your finding without being spotted!

My mission item is:

_____

Was the mission completed without getting caught?

YES   NO

If you were spotted, or the mission was aborted, wait 3 minutes then try again. Nice commitment!

LEVEL 3
MISSION 4
(Expect the unexpected!)

Date:_____ Time:_____

MISSION:

1. Make your way from base to a room or an area.

2. Spy something **COOL**, then return to base and record your finding without being spotted!

My mission item is:

_____

Was the mission completed without getting caught?
YES   NO

If you were spotted, or the mission was aborted, wait 3 minutes then try again. Keep it up!

LEVEL 3
MISSION 5

(Halfway there!)

Date:_____ Time:_____

MISSION:

>1. Make your way from base to a room or an area.

>2. Spy something both **SOFT & SQUARE**, then return to base and record your finding without being spotted!

My mission item is:

_____

Was the mission completed without getting caught?
YES   **NO**

If you were spotted, or the mission was aborted, wait 3 minutes then try again. Halfway there!

LEVEL 3
MISSION 6
(Challenges help you grow!)

Date:_____ **Time:**_____

MISSION:

1. Make your way from base to a room or an area.

2. Spy something that is your **FAVORITE COLOR**, then return to base and record your finding without being spotted!

My mission item is:

_____

Was the mission completed without getting caught?
YES   NO

If you were spotted, or the mission was aborted, wait 3 minutes then try again. Too easy!

LEVEL 3
MISSION 7
(Be proud of yourself!)

Date:_____ Time:_____

MISSION:

1. Make your way from base to a room or an area.

2. Spy something that is **SHINY**, and then return to base and record your finding without being spotted!

My mission item is:

_____

Was the mission completed without getting caught?
YES   NO

If you were spotted, or the mission was aborted, wait 3 minutes then try again. Waiting is a spy skill too!

LEVEL 3
MISSION 8
(Take a chance.)

Date:_____ **Time:**_____

MISSION:

1. Make your way from base to a room or an area.

2. Spy something that **MAKES YOU SMILE** then return to base and record your finding without being spotted!

My mission item is:

_____

Was the mission completed without getting caught?

YES   **NO**

If you were spotted, or the mission was aborted, wait 3 minutes then try again. Spies never give up!

LEVEL 3
MISSION 9
(ALMOST THERE.)

Date:_____ Time:_____

MISSION:

1. Make your way from base to a room or an area.

2. Spy something that **YOU USE TO WRITE,** and then return to base and record your finding without being spotted!

My mission item is:

_____

Was the mission completed without getting caught?
YES   NO

If you were spotted, or the mission was aborted, wait 3 minutes then try again. Breathe!

LEVEL 3
MISSION 10
(WOW.)

Date:_____ **Time:**_____

MISSION:

1. Make your way from base to a room or an area.

2. Spy something that has **BUTTONS,** and then return to base and record your finding without being spotted!

My mission item is:

_____

Was the mission completed without getting caught?

YES   NO

If you were spotted, or the mission was aborted, wait 3 minutes then try again. Keep it up!

CONGRATULATIONS!
You are now a
LEVEL 4 SPY!

LEVEL 4
MISSION 1
(Time to switch things up!)

Date:_____ Time:_____

MISSION (Read Closely):

1. Make your way from base to a room or an area.

2. Spy something that is **SMALL.**

3. Without being seen, **GRAB** it and return to base **WITH** it.

4. Mission is complete, return item.

My mission item is:

_____

Was the mission completed without getting caught?
YES   NO

If you were spotted, or the mission was aborted, wait 3 minutes then try again. Too easy!

LEVEL 4
MISSION 2
(Whew.)

Date:_____ Time:_____

MISSION (Read Closely):

1. Make your way from base to a room or an area.

2. Spy something that is **A LITTLE BIT BIGGER.**

3. Without being seen, **GRAB** it and return to base **WITH** it.

4. Mission is complete, return item.

My mission item is:

_____

Was the mission completed without getting caught?
YES   NO

If you were spotted, or the mission was aborted, wait 3 minutes then try again. Keep Trying!

LEVEL 4
MISSION 3
(Stay Positive.)

Date:_____ Time:_____

MISSION (Read Closely):

1. Make your way from base to a room or an area.

2. Spy something that is **OUT IN THE OPEN.**

3. Without being seen, **GRAB** it and return to base **WITH** it.

4. Mission is complete, return item.

My mission item is:

_____

Was the mission completed without getting caught?
YES   NO

If you were spotted, or the mission was aborted, wait 3 minutes then try again. Spies never quit!

LEVEL 4
MISSION 4
(Don't forget your training.)

Date:_____ **Time:**_____

MISSION (Read Closely):

1. Make your way from base to a room or an area.

2. Spy something that **GOES ON A FOOT.**

3. Without being seen, **GRAB** it and return to base **WITH** it.

4. Mission is complete, return item.

My mission item is:

_____

Was the mission completed without getting caught?

YES   NO

If you were spotted, or the mission was aborted, wait 3 minutes then try again. Waiting is a spy skill too!

LEVEL 4
MISSION 5
(You are so sneaky.)

Date:_____ **Time:**_____

MISSION (Read Closely):

1. Make your way from base to a room or an area.

2. Spy something that **CHANGES THE TV CHANNEL.**

3. Without being seen, **GRAB** it and return to base **WITH** it.

4. Mission is complete, return item.

My mission item is:

_____

Was the mission completed without getting caught?
YES   NO

If you were spotted, or the mission was aborted, wait 3 minutes then try again. Halfway there!

LEVEL 4
MISSION 6
(You are good at hard tasks.)

Date:_____   Time:_____

MISSION (Read Closely):

1. Make your way from base to a room or an area.

2. Spy something that **STIRS (think a spoon or spatula).**

3. Without being seen, **GRAB** it and return to base **WITH** it.

4. Mission is complete, return item.

My mission item is:

_____

Was the mission completed without getting caught?
YES   NO

If you were spotted, or the mission was aborted, wait 3 minutes then try again.

Nice commitment!

LEVEL 4
MISSION 7
(You make the impossible, possible.)

Date:_____ Time:_____

MISSION (Read Closely):

1. Make your way from base to a room or an area.

2. Spy something that is **BRIGHTLY COLORED.**

3. Without being seen, **GRAB** it and return to base **WITH** it.

4. Mission is complete, return item.

My mission item is:

_____

Was the mission completed without getting caught?
YES   NO

If you were spotted, or the mission was aborted, wait 3 minutes then try again. Keep it up!

LEVEL 4
MISSION 8
(Don't forget to breathe.)

Date:_____ Time:_____

MISSION (Read Closely):

1. Make your way from base to a room or an area.

2. Spy something that is **IN A DRAWER.**

3. Without being seen, **GRAB** it and return to base **WITH** it.

4. Mission is complete, return item.

My mission item is:

_____

Was the mission completed without getting caught?
YES   NO

If you were spotted, or the mission was aborted, wait 3 minutes then try again. You got this!

LEVEL 4
MISSION 9
(YOU ROCK.)

Date:_____ **Time:**_____

MISSION (Read Closely):

1. Make your way from base to a room or an area.

2. Spy something that is **IN A CLOSET.**

3. Without being seen, **GRAB** it and return to base **WITH** it.

4. Mission is complete, return item.

My mission item is:

_____

Was the mission completed without getting caught?

YES   NO

If you were spotted, or the mission was aborted, wait 3 minutes then try again. You are so close!

LEVEL 4
MISSION 10
(LAST MISSION.)

Date:_____ Time:_____

MISSION (Read Closely):

    1. Make your way from base to a room or an area.

    2. Spy something that is **CLOSE TO SOMEONE.**

    3. Without being seen, **GRAB** it and return to base **WITH** it.

    4. Mission is complete, return item.

My mission item is:

_____

Was the mission completed without getting caught?

       YES   **NO**

If you were spotted, or the mission was aborted, wait 3 minutes then try again. You got this!!!

CONGRATULATIONS!
You are now a
LEVEL 5 SPY!

SUPER OFFICIAL DEBRIEF

WOW!

You have shown some serious spy skills!

Congratulations! You are now officially part of the Super Secret Spy Group (Triple-S.G. for short). You should be very proud of yourself!

Now that you are an official member, you know how to be even more flexible, creative, brave, and observational. You can overcome hard tasks!

Be sure to fill out your Super Secret Spy Card to keep with you!

DEBRIEF COMPLETE

SUPER SECRET SPY MEMBER

Spy Name: _____

TOP SECRET

SUPER SECRET SPY MEMBER

TOP SECRET

Spy Name:
_____

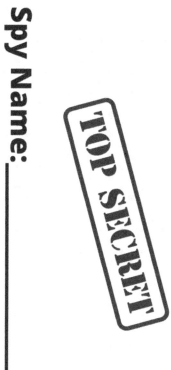

TOP SECRET NOTES

TOP SECRET NOTES

_____

_____

_____

_____

_____

_____

_____

_____

_____

_____

_____

_____

_____

_____

_____

TOP SECRET NOTES

TOP SECRET NOTES

_____

_____

_____

_____

_____

_____

_____

_____

_____

_____

_____

_____

_____

_____

_____

_____

TOP SECRET NOTES

TOP SECRET NOTES

_____

_____

_____

_____

_____

_____

_____

_____

_____

_____

_____

_____

_____

_____

_____

TOP SECRET NOTES

Mission Item Ideas:

- Apple
- Ball
- Block
- Tabletop
- Chocolate bar
- T.V.
- Cell phone
- Baseboard
- Lego
- Straw
- Book
- Velcro
- Box of crackers, cereal, etc.
- Paper
- Glass, Glasses
- Window
- Basketball
- Orange (Like the fruit)
- Ring
- Coin
- Doorknob
- Pillow